Play Ball

Multiplication is a short way to add equal groups.
The **x** sign means to multiply.

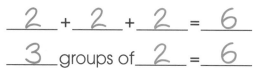

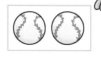 

How many groups? __3__
How many in each group? __2__
How many in all? __6__

__2__ + __2__ + __2__ = __6__
__3__ groups of __2__ = __6__
__3__ x __2__ = __6__

How many?

1.

__5__ + _____ = _____
__2__ groups of __5__ = _____
_____ x __5__ = _____

2.

__3__ + __3__ + _____ + _____ = _____
__4__ groups of _____ = _____
__4__ x _____ = _____

3.

_____ + _____ + _____ = _____
_____ groups of _____ = _____
_____ x _____ = _____

4.

_____ + _____ + _____ + _____ + _____ = _____
_____ groups of _____ = _____
_____ x _____ = _____

Animal Roundup

Use multiplication to describe equal groups.
The **x** sign means to multiply.

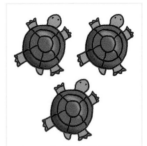

How many groups? __2__

How many in each group? __3__

How many in all? __6__

__2__ x __3__ = __6__

Write a multiplication sentence to find how many.

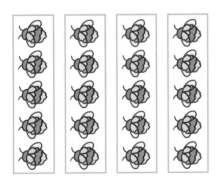

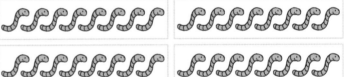

1. _____ x _____ = _____

2. _____ x _____ = _____

3. _____ x _____ = _____

4. _____ x _____ = _____

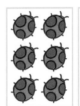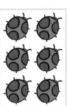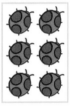

5. _____ x _____ = _____

6. _____ x _____ = _____

© School Zone Publishing Company

Make Snakes

Draw snakes to find how many.

3 x 5 = 15

3 x 5 = _____

Draw groups of snakes for each multiplication problem. Then tell how many in all.

1. 2 x 4 = _____

2. 5 x 3 = _____

3. 2 x 3 = _____

4. 3 x 4 = _____

© School Zone Publishing Company   Understand multiplication: Equal groups

Addition, Addition

Multiplication shows repeated addition of the same addend.

In addition, the answer is called the *sum*. The numbers that are added are called *addends*.

addends → $5 + 5 + 5 + 5 = \underline{20}$ ← sum

In multiplication, the answer is called the *product*. The numbers that are multiplied are called *factors*.

$\underline{4} \times \underline{5} = \underline{20}$

factors   product

Write each addition problem as a multiplication problem. Find each sum and product.

1. $8 + 8 = \underline{\hspace{1cm}}$

   $\underline{2} \times \underline{\hspace{1cm}} = \underline{\hspace{1cm}}$

2. $3 + 3 + 3 + 3 + 3 = \underline{\hspace{1cm}}$

   $\underline{\hspace{1cm}} \times \underline{\hspace{1cm}} = \underline{\hspace{1cm}}$

3. $7 + 7 + 7 + 7 = \underline{\hspace{1cm}}$

   $\underline{\hspace{1cm}} \times \underline{\hspace{1cm}} = \underline{\hspace{1cm}}$

4. $6 + 6 + 6 = \underline{\hspace{1cm}}$

   $\underline{\hspace{1cm}} \times \underline{\hspace{1cm}} = \underline{\hspace{1cm}}$

Write each multiplication problem as an addition problem. Find each product and sum.

5. $5 \times 4 = \underline{\hspace{1cm}}$

   $\underline{\hspace{1cm}} + \underline{\hspace{1cm}} + \underline{\hspace{1cm}} + \underline{\hspace{1cm}} + \underline{\hspace{1cm}} = \underline{\hspace{1cm}}$

6. $3 \times 7 = \underline{\hspace{1cm}}$

   $\underline{\hspace{1cm}} + \underline{\hspace{1cm}} + \underline{\hspace{1cm}} = \underline{\hspace{1cm}}$

7. Why are the sum and the product the same in each problem?

   _____

   _____

© School Zone Publishing Company

You're a Problem Solver

A book of stamps has 2 rows with 4 stamps in each row.
How many stamps are there?

$4 + 4 = 8$

$2 \times 4 = 8$

Answer each problem using repeated addition and multiplication.

1. Ed reads 2 books a week. How many books will be read in 6 weeks?

    _____ + _____ + _____ + _____ + _____ + _____ = _____

    _____ x _____ = _____

2. Maria baby-sits for 4 different families. If each family has 3 children,
    how many children does she baby-sit?

    _____ + _____ + _____ + _____ = _____

    _____ x _____ = _____

3. Kai's dog eats 2 times a day. How many times is the dog fed in 5 days?

    _____ + _____ + _____ + _____ + _____ = _____

    _____ x _____ = _____

4. Four golfers each have 9 golf balls. How many golf balls in all?

    _____ + _____ + _____ + _____ = _____

    _____ x _____ = _____

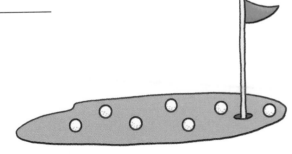

© School Zone Publishing Company

Solve problems using repeated addition and multiplication

Skip on the Line

You can use a number line to help you skip count.

skip, skip, skip on the line...

1. Skip count by twos.

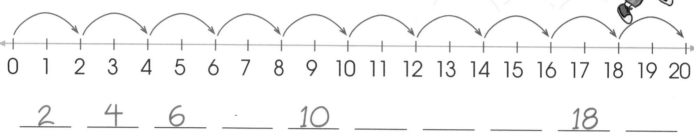

_2_   _4_   _6_   _ _   _10_   _ _   _ _   _ _   _18_   _ _

2. Skip count by threes.

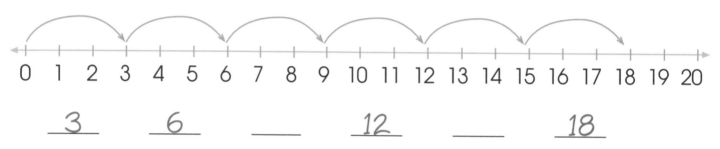

_3_   _6_   _ _   _12_   _ _   _18_

3. Skip count by fours.

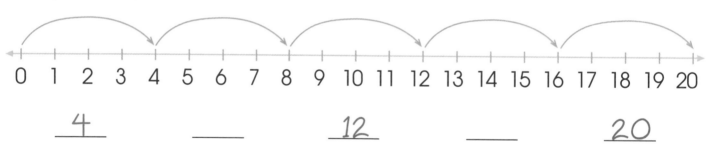

_4_   _ _   _12_   _ _   _20_

4. Skip count by fives.

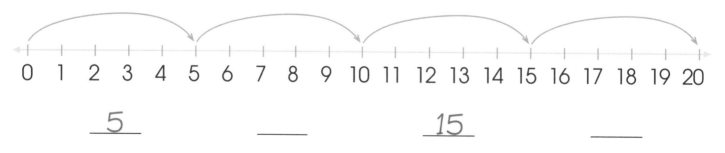

_5_   _ _   _15_   _ _

© School Zone Publishing Company

Skip Count from Dot to Dot

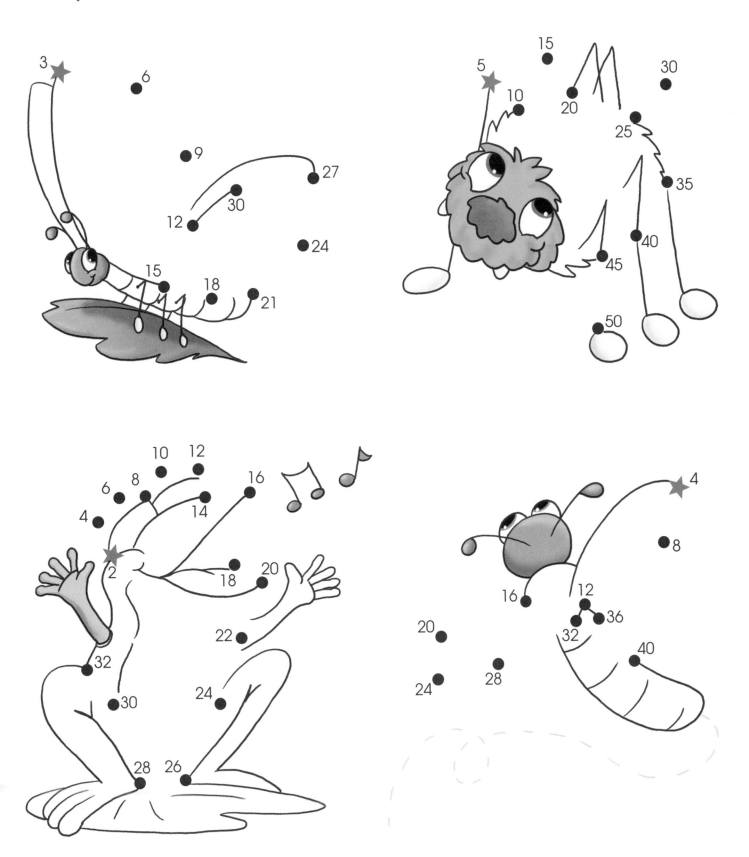

© School Zone Publishing Company

Twice the Fun

When objects are in equal groups, you can skip count to find how many in all.
To multiply by 2, skip count by twos to find the products.

2×1	2×2	2×3	2×4	2×5	2×6	2×7	2×8	2×9
2	4	6	8	10	12	14	16	18

Multiply by 2. Write the product.

1. $2 \times 2 =$ _____

2. $2 \times 8 =$ _____

3. $2 \times 5 =$ _____

4. $2 \times 7 =$ _____

5. $2 \times 1 =$ _____

6. $2 \times 6 =$ _____

7. $2 \times 9 =$ _____

8. $2 \times 3 =$ _____

9. $2 \times 4 =$ _____

Start at the arrow to find the cake. Follow the path in the same order as your answers above.

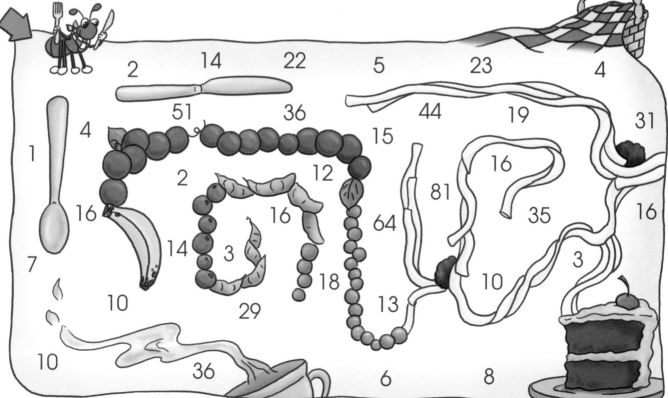

© School Zone Publishing Company

Do the Twos

1. Practice the facts.

2 x 1 = _____

2 x 2 = _____

2 x 3 = _____

2 x 4 = _____

2 x 5 = _____

2 x 6 = _____

2 x 7 = _____

2 x 8 = _____

2 x 9 = _____

2. Practice the facts.

| 4 | 8 | 5 |
| x 2 | x 2 | x 2 |

| 1 | 3 | 2 |
| x 2 | x 2 | x 2 |

| 9 | 6 | 8 |
| x 2 | x 2 | x 2 |

| 7 | 9 | 6 |
| x 2 | x 2 | x 2 |

Count by twos to
check your answers.

3. When you multiply by 2, the product ends with a _2_, _____, _6_, _____, or _0_

4. Complete the table.

x	0	1	2	3	4	5	6	7	8	9
2										

© School Zone Publishing Company

Three's a Breeze

To multiply by 3, skip count by threes to find the product.

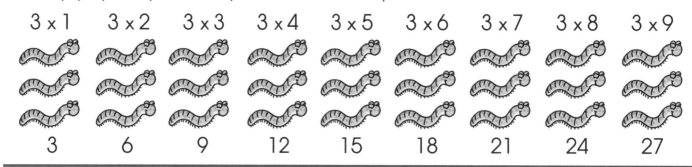

3×1	3×2	3×3	3×4	3×5	3×6	3×7	3×8	3×9
3	6	9	12	15	18	21	24	27

Multiply by 3. Write the product.

1. $3 \times 5 =$ _____

2. $3 \times 1 =$ _____

3. $3 \times 4 =$ _____

4. $3 \times 6 =$ _____

5. $3 \times 8 =$ _____

6. $3 \times 2 =$ _____

7. $3 \times 7 =$ _____

8. $3 \times 9 =$ _____

9. $3 \times 3 =$ _____

Write a multiplication fact for each problem.

10.

_____ x _____ = _____

11.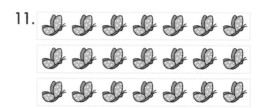

_____ x _____ = _____

12.

_____ x _____ = _____

13.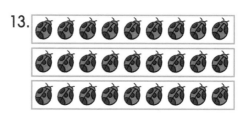

_____ x _____ = _____

© School Zone Publishing Company

Three's Company

1. Practice the facts.

$3 \times 1 =$ _____

$3 \times 2 =$ _____

$3 \times 3 =$ _____

$3 \times 4 =$ _____

$3 \times 5 =$ _____

$3 \times 6 =$ _____

$3 \times 7 =$ _____

$3 \times 8 =$ _____

$3 \times 9 =$ _____

2. Practice the facts.

$$\begin{array}{r} 5 \\ \times\ 3 \\ \hline \end{array} \qquad \begin{array}{r} 8 \\ \times\ 3 \\ \hline \end{array} \qquad \begin{array}{r} 4 \\ \times\ 3 \\ \hline \end{array}$$

$$\begin{array}{r} 2 \\ \times\ 3 \\ \hline \end{array} \qquad \begin{array}{r} 1 \\ \times\ 3 \\ \hline \end{array} \qquad \begin{array}{r} 2 \\ \times\ 3 \\ \hline \end{array}$$

$$\begin{array}{r} 6 \\ \times\ 3 \\ \hline \end{array} \qquad \begin{array}{r} 9 \\ \times\ 3 \\ \hline \end{array} \qquad \begin{array}{r} 8 \\ \times\ 3 \\ \hline \end{array}$$

$$\begin{array}{r} 9 \\ \times\ 3 \\ \hline \end{array} \qquad \begin{array}{r} 7 \\ \times\ 3 \\ \hline \end{array} \qquad \begin{array}{r} 6 \\ \times\ 3 \\ \hline \end{array}$$

Count by threes to
check your answers.

Complete the tables.

3.

x	0	1	2	3	4	5	6	7	8	9
3										

4.

x	6	3	1	0	2	7	4	9	5	8
3										

© School Zone Publishing Company

What's an Array?

An **array** shows objects in rows and columns. When an array is used with multiplication, one factor is the number of rows. The other factor is the number of columns.

4 columns

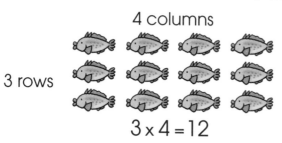

3 rows

$$3 \times 4 = 12$$

You can count all the objects in the array to make sure you have the correct answer.

Write a multiplication sentence to describe each array.

1.

_____ x _____ = _____
  rows   columns

2.

_____ x _____ = _____

3.

_____ x _____ = _____

4.

_____ x _____ = _____

5.

_____ x _____ = _____

6.

_____ x _____ = _____

Circle the pictures that show arrays. Write a multiplication sentence for each array.

7.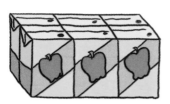

_____

8.

_____

9.

_____

© School Zone Publishing Company

Display Arrays

To show an array, draw objects in neat rows and columns.

Multiply by 3 x 7

____3____ rows of ___7___

___3___ x ___7___ = _21_

Draw an array to find each product.

1. 2 x 6 = _____

2. 4 x 5 = _____

3. 5 x 3 = _____

4. 3 x 9 = _____

5. 2 x 8 = _____

6. 4 x 6 = _____

© School Zone Publishing Company   Understand multiplication: Use arrays

Explore the Fours

Use arrays to help you learn these multiplication facts.

Multiply by 4 x 6

___4___ rows of ___6___

___4___ x ___6___ = ___24___

Write a multiplication sentence for each array.

1.

___4___ rows of _____

_____ x _____ = _____

2.

_____ rows of _____

_____ x _____ = _____

4. Practice the facts.

5	3	1	7	6	9	4	8
x 4	x 4	x 4	x 4	x 4	x 4	x 4	x 4

3. Practice the facts.

4 x 1 = _____

4 x 2 = _____

4 x 3 = _____

4 x 4 = _____

4 x 5 = _____

4 x 6 = _____

4 x 7 = _____

4 x 8 = _____

4 x 9 = _____

Count by fours to
Check your answers.

© School Zone Publishing Company

Serving Up a Riddle

Multiply.

I

1. 1
    x 4

N

2. 3
    x 4

L

3. 7
    x 4

A

3. 5
    x 4

E

4. 9
    x 4

B

5. 4
    x 4

T

7. 6
    x 4

L

8. 7
    x 4

S

9. 2
    x 4

Use your answers to decode the riddle below.
Write the letter for each answer on the correct blank.

What can you serve but never eat?

___ ___ ___ ___ ___ ___ ___ ___ ___ ___ ___
20   24 36 12 12 4   8   16 20 28 28

10. Complete the table.

x	0	1	2	3	4	5	6	7	8	9
4										

© School Zone Publishing Company

Save Your Nickels

A nickel is worth 5¢. You can skip count to find the total amount.

5¢   10¢   15¢   20¢   25¢   30¢   6 x 5¢ = __30¢__

Count the nickels. Fill in the missing numbers.

1.   _____ x 5¢ = _____ ¢

2.   _____ x 5¢ = _____ ¢

3.   _____ x 5¢ = _____ ¢

4.   _____ x 5¢ = _____ ¢

5.   _____ x 5¢ = _____ ¢

6.

          _____ x 5¢ = _____ ¢

© School Zone Publishing Company

Five Alive!

5...   10...   15...   20...

1. Practice the facts.

5 x 1 = _____

5 x 2 = _____

5 x 3 = _____

5 x 4 = _____

5 x 5 = _____

5 x 6 = _____

5 x 7 = _____

5 x 8 = _____

5 x 9 = _____

Count by fives to
check your answers.

2. Practice the facts.

```
    3         1         5
  x 5       x 5       x 5
```

```
    8         6         2
  x 5       x 5       x 5
```

```
    7         5         4
  x 5       x 6       x 5
```

```
    9         5         5
  x 5       x 4       x 7
```

3. When you multiply by 5, the product ends with a _____ or _____ .

4. Complete the table.

x	0	1	2	3	4	5	6	7	8	9
5										

© School Zone Publishing Company

Skip Ahead!

Skip count to finish each pattern.

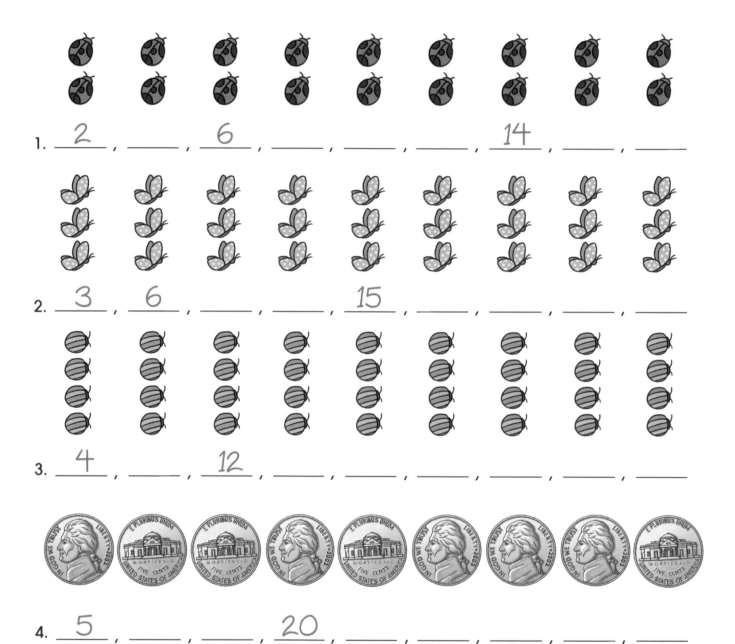

1. ___2___ , _____ , ___6___ , _____ , _____ , _____ , ___14___ , _____ , _____

2. ___3___ , ___6___ , _____ , _____ , ___15___ , _____ , _____ , _____ , _____

3. ___4___ , _____ , ___12___ , _____ , _____ , _____ , _____ , _____ , _____

4. ___5___ , _____ , _____ , ___20___ , _____ , _____ , _____ , _____ , _____

5. ___10___ , _____ , ___30___ , _____ , _____ , _____ , _____ , _____ , _____

© School Zone Publishing Company

Quick Count

Circle groups of 5. Then skip count.

1. ___5___ , ___10___ , _____ , _____ , _____

Circle groups of 4. Then skip count.

2. ___4___ , _____ , _____ , ___16___

Circle groups of 2. Then skip count.

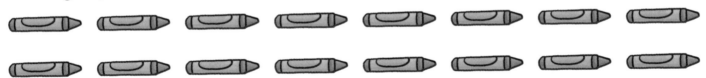

3. ___2___ , _____ , _____ , ___10___ , _____ , _____ , _____

Circle groups of 3. Then skip count.

4. ___3___ , _____ , _____ , ___12___ , _____

© School Zone Publishing Company

In Any Order

You can multiply factors in any order and get the same product.

How many?

How many?

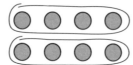

$2 \times 4 = 8$

How many?

$4 \times 2 = 8$

Write a multiplication sentence for each array.

1.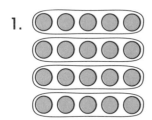

___4___ x _____ = _____

2.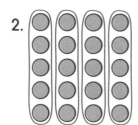

___5___ x _____ = _____

3.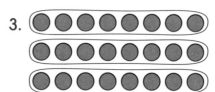

_____ x _____ = _____

4.

_____ x _____ = _____

5.

_____ x _____ = _____

6.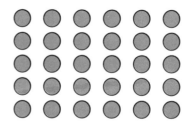

_____ x _____ = _____

Draw circles around the rows or columns in the array to show the multiplication problem. Then write the product.

7. $3 \times 6 =$ _____

8. $5 \times 4 =$ _____

9. $6 \times 5 =$ _____

© School Zone Publishing Company

Draw a Winner

When two numbers are multiplied, they can be in any order. The products are the same.

3 groups of 2

   $3 \times 2 = 6$

2 groups of 3

   $2 \times 3 = 6$

Draw groups of s to show each problem. Then write the product.

1. $4 \times 2 = $ _____

2. $2 \times 4 = $ _____

3. $5 \times 3 = $ _____

4. $3 \times 5 = $ _____

5. $3 \times 4 = $ _____

6. $4 \times 3 = $ _____

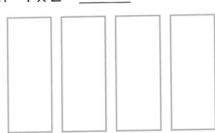

© School Zone Publishing Company

Multiply by 1 and 0

Any number times 1 equals that number.   Any number times 0 equals 0.

1 group of 3 = 3   3 groups of 1 = 3   3 group of 0 = 0   0 groups of 3 = 0
1 x 3 = 3   3 x 1 = 3   3 x 0 = 0   0 x 3 = 0

Count the number in each group. Multiply to find the answer.

1.
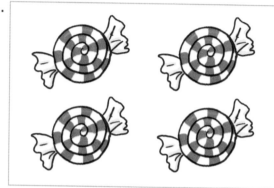

2.

How many groups? _____   How many groups? _____

How many in each group? _____   How many in each group? _____

_____ x _____ = _____   _____ x _____ = _____

Multiply.

3. 1 x 8 = _____   4. 4 x 1 = _____   5. 0 x 5 = _____

6. 8 x 0 = _____   7. 1 x 7 = _____   8. 0 x 4 = _____

9. 6 x 1 = _____   10. 0 x 7 = _____   11. 3 x 0 = _____

© School Zone Publishing Company

Easy Ones!

1. Complete the table.

x	0	1	2	3	4	5	6	7	8	9
0										
1										

2. Any number times 0 equals _____ .

3. Any number times 1 equals _____ .

4. Practice the facts.

1 x 3 = _____

5 x 1 = _____

1 x 8 = _____

6 x 1 = _____

1 x 4 = _____

9 x 1 = _____

5. Practice the facts.

0 x 3 = _____

4 x 0 = _____

0 x 8 = _____

7 x 0 = _____

0 x 9 = _____

0 x 0 = _____

6. Practice the facts.

```
   5        3        1        0        6        9        4        8
 x 1      x 0      x 4      x 4      x 0      x 1      x 0      x 1
```

7. Try these!

```
  25       37       43       97       60       99       74       82
 x 0      x 1      x 1      x 0      x 1      x 0      x 1      x 0
```

© School Zone Publishing Company

Try a Table

You can use a multiplication table to learn new facts and to find products.

In $4 \times 2 =$ _____ , the factors are 4 and 2.

The factors are shown in the top row and in the first column.

Step 1: Find the 4 row and look to the right.

Step 2: Find the 2 column and look down.

Step 3: Find where the 4 row and the 2 column meet. That is the product.

$4 \times 2 = 8$

X	0	1	2	3	4	5
0	0	0	0	0	0	0
1	0	1	2	3	4	5
2	0	2	4	6	8	10
3	0	3	6	9	12	15
4	0	4	8	12	16	20
5	0	5	10	15	20	25

Name the factors. Then use the multiplication table to find the product.

	Factors	Product
1. 3×2	_____ _____	_____
2. 5×5	_____ _____	_____
3. 0×1	_____ _____	_____
4. 2×4	_____ _____	_____
5. 5×0	_____ _____	_____
6. 4×3	_____ _____	_____
7. 3×3	_____ _____	_____
8. 1×5	_____ _____	_____

© School Zone Publishing Company

It's in the Table!

1. Complete the table.

x	0	1	2	3	4	5	6	7	8	9
0	0	0					0			
1					4			7		
2							12			
3						15				
4	0								32	
5		5								

Look for patterns in the table.

2. Look at the **2** row.
When you multiply by 2, the product ends in _____, _____, _____, _____, or _____.

3. Look at the **5** row.
When you multiply by 5, the product ends in _____ or _____.

4. Look at the **0** row. What is each product? _____

5. Look at the **1** row. What do you notice about each product? _____

6. Multiply: 3 x 5 = _____ and 5 x 3 = _____   3 x 2 = _____ and 2 x 3 = _____

Why are the products the same for each pair of facts? _____

Know the Facts

Multiply.

© School Zone Publishing Company

Multiplication Art

1. How many buttons are on the coat? _____

   How many buttons would there be on 7 coats? _____   on 4 coats? _____

2. How many red stripes are on the hat? _____

   How many red stripes would there be on 5 hats? _____   on 9 hats? _____

3. How many patches are on the pants? _____

   How many patches would there be on 8 pants? _____   on 6 pants? _____

© School Zone Publishing Company   Practice multiplication facts

Gopher It!

Multiply by 6.

6 x 1	6 x 2	6 x 3	6 x 4	6 x 5	6 x 6	6 x 7	6 x 8	6 x 9

6	12	18	24	30	36	42	48	54

Help the gopher find it's way home. Multiply and then color the even number products. (Even numbers end in 2, 4, 6, 8, or 0.)

6 x 4	3 x 3	6 x 9	3 x 6	6 x 7
6 x 6	5 x 9	0 x 6	3 x 9	1 x 6
4 x 6	1 x 7	5 x 6	5 x 7	6 x 9
2 x 6	6 x 3	6 x 8	1 x 9	6 x 2

Complete the table.

x	0	1	2	3	4	5	6	7	8	9
6										

© School Zone Publishing Company

Fiddlesticks! It's Six!

Write a multiplication sentence for each array.

1.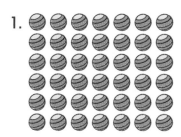

___6___ rows of _____

_____ x _____ = _____

2.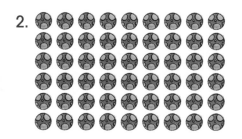

_____ rows of _____

_____ x _____ = _____

3. Practice the facts.

6 x 1 = _____

6 x 2 = _____

6 x 3 = _____

6 x 4 = _____

6 x 5 = _____

6 x 6 = _____

6 x 7 = _____

6 x 8 = _____

6 x 9 = _____

Count by sixes to
check your answers.

4. Practice the facts.

5	6	1	7	6	9	6	8
x 6	x 4	x 6	x 6	x 8	x 6	x 3	x 6

© School Zone Publishing Company

Lucky Seven

You can use multiplication facts that you already know to learn new facts.

$7 \times 8 =$ _____

$2 \times 8 = 16$
and
$5 \times 8 = 40$
equals
$7 \times 8 = 56$

---

1. $7 \times 5 = \underline{2} \times 5 =$ _____

   and _____ $\times 5 =$ _____

   So, $7 \times 5 =$ _____

2. $7 \times 7 = \underline{3} \times 7 =$ _____

   and _____ $\times 7 =$ _____

   So, $7 \times 7 =$ _____

3. $7 \times 9 = \underline{4} \times 9 =$ _____

   and _____ $\times$ _____ $=$ _____

   So, $7 \times 9 =$ _____

4. Practice the facts.

   $7 \times 1 =$ _____

   $7 \times 2 =$ _____

   $7 \times 3 =$ _____

   $7 \times 4 =$ _____

   $7 \times 5 =$ _____

   $7 \times 6 =$ _____

   $7 \times 7 =$ _____

   $7 \times 8 =$ _____

   $7 \times 9 =$ _____

5. Practice the facts.

$$\begin{array}{r} 4 \\ \times\ 7 \\ \hline \end{array} \qquad \begin{array}{r} 3 \\ \times\ 7 \\ \hline \end{array} \qquad \begin{array}{r} 7 \\ \times\ 5 \\ \hline \end{array}$$

$$\begin{array}{r} 1 \\ \times\ 7 \\ \hline \end{array} \qquad \begin{array}{r} 7 \\ \times\ 2 \\ \hline \end{array} \qquad \begin{array}{r} 7 \\ \times\ 6 \\ \hline \end{array}$$

$$\begin{array}{r} 9 \\ \times\ 7 \\ \hline \end{array} \qquad \begin{array}{r} 6 \\ \times\ 7 \\ \hline \end{array} \qquad \begin{array}{r} 8 \\ \times\ 7 \\ \hline \end{array}$$

$$\begin{array}{r} 0 \\ \times\ 7 \\ \hline \end{array} \qquad \begin{array}{r} 7 \\ \times\ 8 \\ \hline \end{array} \qquad \begin{array}{r} 2 \\ \times\ 7 \\ \hline \end{array}$$

Count by sevens to
check your answers.

Beans   Peas   Strawberries

© School Zone Publishing Company

The Richest Fish

Multiply.

1. $7 \times 4 =$ _____ **F**

2. $7 \times 9 =$ _____ **L**

3. $7 \times 2 =$ _____ **H**

4. $7 \times 6 =$ _____ **O**

5. $7 \times 3 =$ _____ **S**

6. $7 \times 5 =$ _____ **I**

7. $7 \times 0 =$ _____ **A**

8. $7 \times 8 =$ _____ **G**

9. $7 \times 7 =$ _____ **D**

Use your answers to decode the riddle below.
Write the letter for each answer on the correct blank.

What is the richest fish?

___   ___   ___   ___   ___   ___   ___   ___   ___
0   56   42   63   49   28   35   21   14

10. Complete the table.

x	0	1	2	3	4	5	6	7	8	9
7										

© School Zone Publishing Company

Find the Facts

Multiply to find the product for each problem. Look across and down to find the problems and products in the number search.

1. 4 x 3 = __12__

2. 8 x 0 = _____

3. 2 x 8 = _____

4. 7 x 2 = _____

5. 5 x 4 = _____

6. 3 x 9 = _____

7. 6 x 4 = _____

8. 7 x 9 = _____

9. 5 x 5 = _____

10. 6 x 6 = _____

11. 4 x 7 = _____

12. 3 x 5 = _____

4	0	6	6	36	10	2	41
3	5	15	11	72	26	8	3
12	37	7	2	14	0	16	22
1	5	15	41	7	4	7	28
6	4	24	3	9	27	8	13
53	20	7	18	63	5	0	7
1	12	5	5	25	9	0	34

Multiply to complete each table.

Number of Frogs	Number of Legs
2	8
3	
4	
5	
6	
7	

Number of Flies	Number of Legs
2	12
3	
4	
5	
6	
7	

How do you know that a fly has 6 legs?

ALL insects have 6 legs!

© School Zone Publishing Company

Products in a Pyramid

Multiply. Write the products in the puzzle.

Across

1. 7 x 5 = __35__

2. 4 x 4 = _____

3. 7 x 8 = _____

5. 3 x 8 = _____

6. 4 x 8 = _____

8. 6 x 8 = _____

9. 2 x 7 = _____

11. 8 x 4 = _____

12. 7 x 0 = _____

Down

1. 4 x 9 = _____

2. 2 x 7 = _____

4. 7 x 9 = _____

5. 4 x 7 = _____

7. 3 x 7 = _____

8. 7 x 6 = _____

10. 5 x 8 = _____

© School Zone Publishing Company

Double the Fours

If you know the 4 facts, you can double those products to learn the 8 facts.

Use the facts you know.

$8 \times 9 = \underline{\hphantom{000}}$

$4 \times 9 = 36$

and

$4 \times 9 = 36$

equals

$8 \times 9 = 72$

Write a pair of 4 facts you know to help you find these products.

1. $8 \times 6 = \underline{4} \times 6 = \underline{\hphantom{000}}$

   and $\underline{\hphantom{00}} \times 6 = \underline{\hphantom{000}}$

   So, $8 \times 6 = \underline{\hphantom{000}}$

2. $8 \times 7 = \underline{4} \times 7 = \underline{\hphantom{000}}$

   and $\underline{\hphantom{00}} \times 7 = \underline{\hphantom{000}}$

   So, $8 \times 7 = \underline{\hphantom{000}}$

3. $8 \times 8 = \underline{4} \times 8 = \underline{\hphantom{000}}$

   and $\underline{\hphantom{00}} \times \underline{\hphantom{00}} = \underline{\hphantom{000}}$

   So, $8 \times 8 = \underline{\hphantom{000}}$

4. Practice the facts.

$8 \times 1 = \underline{\hphantom{000}}$

$8 \times 2 = \underline{\hphantom{000}}$

$8 \times 3 = \underline{\hphantom{000}}$

$8 \times 4 = \underline{\hphantom{000}}$

$8 \times 5 = \underline{\hphantom{000}}$

$8 \times 6 = \underline{\hphantom{000}}$

$8 \times 7 = \underline{\hphantom{000}}$

$8 \times 8 = \underline{\hphantom{000}}$

$8 \times 9 = \underline{\hphantom{000}}$

5. Practice the facts.

$\begin{array}{r} 3 \\ \times\ 8 \\ \hline \end{array}$	$\begin{array}{r} 5 \\ \times\ 8 \\ \hline \end{array}$	$\begin{array}{r} 8 \\ \times\ 2 \\ \hline \end{array}$
$\begin{array}{r} 8 \\ \times\ 7 \\ \hline \end{array}$	$\begin{array}{r} 1 \\ \times\ 8 \\ \hline \end{array}$	$\begin{array}{r} 7 \\ \times\ 8 \\ \hline \end{array}$
$\begin{array}{r} 9 \\ \times\ 8 \\ \hline \end{array}$	$\begin{array}{r} 6 \\ \times\ 8 \\ \hline \end{array}$	$\begin{array}{r} 8 \\ \times\ 9 \\ \hline \end{array}$
$\begin{array}{r} 8 \\ \times\ 6 \\ \hline \end{array}$	$\begin{array}{r} 0 \\ \times\ 8 \\ \hline \end{array}$	$\begin{array}{r} 4 \\ \times\ 8 \\ \hline \end{array}$

Count by eights to
check your answers.

© School Zone Publishing Company

Eight Is Great

Multiply.

1. 8 x 3 = _____ **E**

2. 8 x 6 = _____ **L**

3. 8 x 4 = _____ **P**

4. 8 x 8 = _____ **B**

5. 8 x 1 = _____ **A**

6. 8 x 9 = _____ **Y**

7. 8 x 5 = _____ **H**

8. 8 x 7 = _____ **N**

9. 8 x 2 = _____ **T**

Use your answers to decode the riddle below.
Write the letter for each answer on the correct blank.

What does an elephant have that no other animals have?

A __ __ __ __   __ __ __ __ __ __ __ __
   64 8 64 72   24 48 24 32 40 8 56 16

10. Complete the table.

x	0	1	2	3	4	5	6	7	8	9
8										

© School Zone Publishing Company

Nine Is Fine

When you multiply 9 by a single digit, the sum of the digits of the product is 9.

$2 \times 9 = ?$ □□□□□□□□□
             □□□□□□□□□ $2 \times 9 = 18 \longrightarrow 1 + 8 = 9$

$5 \times 9 = ?$ ○○○○○○○○○
             ○○○○○○○○○
             ○○○○○○○○○ $5 \times 9 = 45 \longrightarrow 4 + 5 = 9$
             ○○○○○○○○○
             ○○○○○○○○○

Multiply. Add the digits of the product to check your answer.

1. $9 \times 4 = $ __36__ $\longrightarrow$ __3__ + __6__ = __9__

2. $9 \times 7 = $ _____ $\longrightarrow$ _____ + _____ = _____

3. $9 \times 3 = $ _____ $\longrightarrow$ _____ + _____ = _____

4. $9 \times 8 = $ _____ $\longrightarrow$ _____ + _____ = _____

5. $9 \times 5 = $ _____ $\longrightarrow$ _____ + _____ = _____

6. $9 \times 6 = $ _____ $\longrightarrow$ _____ + _____ = _____

7. $9 \times 9 = $ _____ $\longrightarrow$ _____ + _____ = _____

8. Complete the table.

x	0	1	2	3	4	5	6	7	8	9
9										

© School Zone Publishing Company

Find Nines

Multiply.

1.

3 x 9	5 x 9	7 x 9	1 x 9	8 x 9	0 x 9	6 x 9	2 x 9

2.

4 x 9	9 x 6	9 x 3	9 x 0	9 x 5	9 x 7	9 x 9	9 x 8

Start at the arrow to find the carrot. Follow the path in the same order as your answers above.

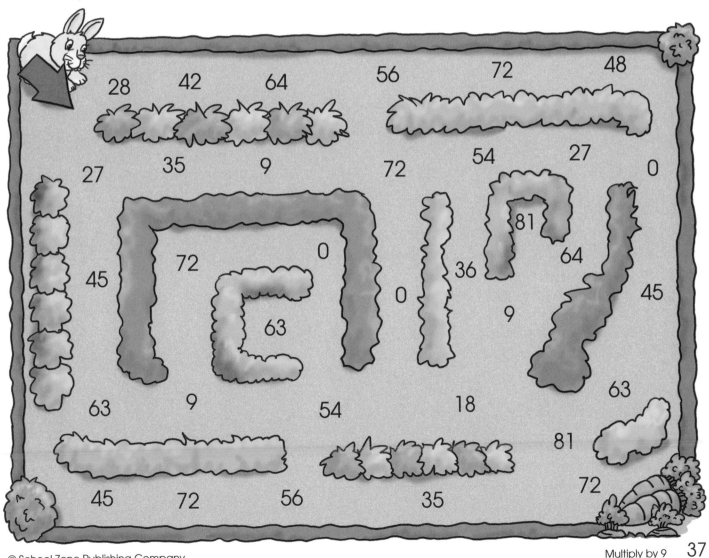

© School Zone Publishing Company

Home Run Riddle

Complete the multiplication table.

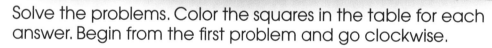

The first factor is the row, and the second factor is the column.

X	0	1	2	3	4	5	6	7	8	9
0		0						0		
1				3						
2	0							14		
3										27
4		4								
5						25				
6	0									
7					28					63
8										
9							54			

Solve the problems. Color the squares in the table for each answer. Begin from the first problem and go clockwise.

1. 7 x 4
2. 3 x 6
3. 4 x 3
4. 5 x 8

5. 2 x 5
6. 6 x 3
7. 8 x 5
8. 4 x 7

9. 3 x 4
10. 7 x 6
11. 5 x 2
12. 6 x 7

Which gem has something in common with baseball?

_____

© School Zone Publishing Company

Cross Out!

When two numbers are multiplied, they can be in any order. The answers will be the same.

$4 \times 3 = 12$ $3 \times 4 = 12$

Multiply. Use a straight edge to draw lines that connect the matching problems. To answer the riddle, write the letters from top to bottom that aren't crossed out.

$7 \times 9 =$ _____ •

R   W

            T

      I

            N

$6 \times 8 =$ _____ •

$8 \times 7 =$ _____ •

S

      D   E

$8 \times 0 =$ _____ •

      A

$5 \times 7 =$ _____ •

                  O

$9 \times 6 =$ _____ •

      W

            P

$7 \times 6 =$ _____ •   C

            M

$8 \times 9 =$ _____ •   S

• $0 \times 8 =$ _____

• $9 \times 7 =$ _____

• $6 \times 9 =$ _____

• $7 \times 5 =$ _____

• $8 \times 6 =$ _____

• $9 \times 8 =$ _____

• $6 \times 7 =$ _____

• $7 \times 8 =$ _____

What invention allows you to see through walls?

____ ____ ____ ____ ____ ____ ____

© School Zone Publishing Company

Commutative (order) property of multiplication   39

Out of This World

Multiply. Use your answers to color the picture.

$7 \times 9 = \underline{\hspace{1cm}}$

$\begin{array}{r} 9 \\ \times\ 6 \\ \hline \end{array}$

$4 \times 9 = \underline{\hspace{1cm}}$

$\begin{array}{r} 3 \\ \times\ 1 \\ \hline \end{array}$

$\begin{array}{r} 0 \\ \times\ 7 \\ \hline \end{array}$

$\begin{array}{r} 8 \\ \times\ 8 \\ \hline \end{array}$

$\begin{array}{r} 8 \\ \times\ 9 \\ \hline \end{array}$

$\begin{array}{r} 5 \\ \times\ 6 \\ \hline \end{array}$

$\begin{array}{r} 9 \\ \times\ 9 \\ \hline \end{array}$

$\begin{array}{r} 4 \\ \times\ 0 \\ \hline \end{array}$

$\begin{array}{r} 6 \\ \times\ 6 \\ \hline \end{array}$

$8 \times 7 = \underline{\hspace{1cm}}$

$\begin{array}{r} 7 \\ \times\ 7 \\ \hline \end{array}$

$\begin{array}{r} 7 \\ \times\ 5 \\ \hline \end{array}$

$8 \times 6 = \underline{\hspace{1cm}}$

$\begin{array}{r} 3 \\ \times\ 8 \\ \hline \end{array}$

$\begin{array}{r} 9 \\ \times\ 3 \\ \hline \end{array}$

$\begin{array}{r} 4 \\ \times\ 4 \\ \hline \end{array}$

$\begin{array}{r} 0 \\ \times\ 8 \\ \hline \end{array}$

$6 \times 3 = \underline{\hspace{1cm}}$

0

1-29

30-49

50-81

Practice multiplication facts 0-9

© School Zone Publishing Company

Bunches of Facts

Write all the multiplication facts that have the following products. A pair of facts like
3 x 4 = 12 and 4 x 3 = 12 will count as one fact since they have the same factors.

1. Products 10-19:

_____, _____, _____, _____,

_____, _____, _____, _____, _____

2. Products 20-29:

_____, _____, _____, _____,

_____, _____, _____

3. Products 30-39:

_____, _____, _____, _____

4. Products 40-49:

_____, _____, _____, _____

5. Products 50-59:

_____, _____

6. Products 60-69:

_____, _____

7. Products 70-79:

_____

8. Products 80-89:

_____

Look! It's easy to remember these facts. There are only one or two facts in each bunch.

Triangle Times

Write a product in each circle.

Practice multiplication facts 0-9

© School Zone Publishing Company

Fast Facts!

Time yourself. Can you do all of these in less than 5 minutes?

1. 2 x 8 = _____   4 x 5 = _____   6 x 4 = _____   3 x 7 = _____

2. 5 x 3 = _____   3 x 8 = _____   5 x 5 = _____   4 x 8 = _____

3. 7 x 4 = _____   4 x 9 = _____   7 x 3 = _____   8 x 6 = _____

4. 5 x 9 = _____   6 x 1 = _____   2 x 9 = _____   4 x 9 = _____

5. 8 x 3 = _____   7 x 2 = _____   5 x 8 = _____   8 x 7 = _____

6. 7 x 9 = _____   8 x 8 = _____   3 x 6 = _____   0 x 9 = _____

7. 4 x 7 = _____   9 x 6 = _____   6 x 8 = _____   9 x 7 = _____

8. 9 x 9 = _____   3 x 0 = _____   8 x 4 = _____   6 x 9 = _____

9. 5 x 8 = _____   7 x 7 = _____   4 x 6 = _____   7 x 8 = _____

10. 9 x 5 = _____   5 x 7 = _____   8 x 0 = _____   9 x 8 = _____

11. 4 x 4 = _____   7 x 6 = _____   5 x 9 = _____   7 x 4 = _____

12. 9 x 3 = _____   0 x 7 = _____   8 x 9 = _____   0 x 0 = _____

© School Zone Publishing Company   Practice multiplication facts 0-9

Bright Idea

In multiplication, the numbers that are multiplied are called **factors**.

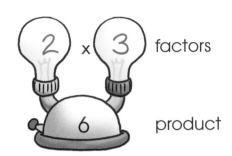

2 x 3 factors

6 product

Write a factor on each light bulb so that the pair of factors equals the product shown.
Use the numbers 2–9 as factors.

1.  x 8

2.  x 12

3.  x 28

4.  x 15

5.  x 18

6.  x 32

7.  x 16

8.  x 21

Multiply.

9. $7 \times 4 =$ _____ V

10. $8 \times 3 =$ _____ A

11. $9 \times 5 =$ _____ I

12. $6 \times 6 =$ _____ R

13. $8 \times 6 =$ _____ R

14. $2 \times 4 =$ _____ E

Use your answers to decode the riddle below.
Write the letter for each answer on the correct blank.

What has a big mouth but doesn't say a word?

___ ___ ___ ___ ___ ___
24   36   45   28   8   48

© School Zone Publishing Company

What's Missing?

Find the missing factors.

$$\begin{array}{r} 3 \\ \times \boxed{?} \\ \hline 15 \end{array}$$

3 times what number equals 15?

$$\begin{array}{r} 3 \\ \times \boxed{5} \\ \hline 15 \end{array}$$

Write the missing factor for each number sentence.

Y

1. $$\begin{array}{r} 4 \\ \times \boxed{} \\ \hline 20 \end{array}$$

A

2. $$\begin{array}{r} \boxed{} \\ \times \ 8 \\ \hline 48 \end{array}$$

I

3. $$\begin{array}{r} 5 \\ \times \boxed{} \\ \hline 45 \end{array}$$

A

4. $$\begin{array}{r} \boxed{} \\ \times \ 7 \\ \hline 42 \end{array}$$

N

5. $$\begin{array}{r} 8 \\ \times \boxed{} \\ \hline 16 \end{array}$$

L

6. $$\begin{array}{r} \boxed{} \\ \times \ 8 \\ \hline 24 \end{array}$$

F

7. $$\begin{array}{r} 9 \\ \times \boxed{} \\ \hline 63 \end{array}$$

G

8. $$\begin{array}{r} 3 \\ \times \boxed{} \\ \hline 12 \end{array}$$

Z

9. $$\begin{array}{r} 5 \\ \times \boxed{} \\ \hline 40 \end{array}$$

I

10. $$\begin{array}{r} \boxed{} \\ \times \ 4 \\ \hline 36 \end{array}$$

P

11. $$\begin{array}{r} 4 \\ \times \boxed{} \\ \hline 4 \end{array}$$

Z

12. $$\begin{array}{r} \boxed{} \\ \times \ 7 \\ \hline 56 \end{array}$$

Use the numbers you wrote to decode the riddle below.
Write the letter for each number on the correct blank.

What is a pie in the sky?

__ __ __ __ __ __ __   __ __ __ __ __
6   7   3   5   9   2   4   1   9   8   8   6

© School Zone Publishing Company

Dime Time

A dime is worth 10¢. You can skip-count to find the total amount.

10¢   20¢   30¢   40¢   50¢

5 x 10¢ = <u>50¢</u>

Count the dimes. Fill in the missing numbers.

1.   ____ x 10¢ = ____¢

2.   ____ x 10¢ = ____¢

3.   ____ x 10¢ = ____¢

4.   ____ x 10¢ = ____¢

5.   ____ x 10¢ = ____¢

6.

   ____ x 10¢ = ____¢

© School Zone Publishing Company

Ten Again

1. Practice the facts.

10 x 1 = _____

10 x 2 = _____

10 x 3 = _____

10 x 4 = _____

10 x 5 = _____

10 x 6 = _____

10 x 7 = _____

10 x 8 = _____

10 x 9 = _____

Count by tens to
check you answers.

2. Practice the facts.

10 x 6 = _____

10 x 4 = _____

1 x 10 = _____

10 x 3 = _____

5 x 10 = _____

10 x 8 = _____

7 x 10 = _____

10 x 0 = _____

2 x 10 = _____

9 x 10 = _____

3. When you multiply a number times 10, the product
ends with a _____.

4. Complete the table.

x	0	1	2	3	4	5	6	7	8	9
10										

5. Try These!

10 x 10 = _____   10 x 11 = _____   10 x 12 = _____

© School Zone Publishing Company

Double-Digit Time

To multiply by 11 times a number from 1 through 9, remember this clue.
The product is a two-digit number that repeats the factor.

11 x 1	11 x 2	11 x 3	11 x 4	11 x 5	11 x 6	11 x 7	11 x 8	11 x 9
11	22	33	44	55	66	77	88	99

Look across and down to find the problems and products in the number search.

1. 11 x 3 = <u>33</u>   2. 11 x 7 = _____

3. 11 x 9 = _____   4. 11 x 4 = _____

5. 11 x 2 = _____   6. 11 x 8 = _____

7. 11 x 5 = _____   8. 11 x 1 = _____

9. 11 x 0 = _____   10. 11 x 6 = _____

11	17	1	28	11	7	77
5	11	4	44	16	48	11
55	32	63	11	0	0	3
0	11	8	88	11	38	33
24	9	56	71	1	15	41
65	99	36	23	11	2	22
18	11	6	66	43	0	17

Complete the table.

x	0	1	2	3	4	5	6	7	8	9
11										

© School Zone Publishing Company

Ten and One

Here is another way to learn the 11 facts. Since 11 = 10 + 1.
Complete the pattern to find any number multiplied by 11.

11 x 1 = (10 x 1) + 1

    = __10__ + 1 = _____

11 x 2 = (10 x 2) + 2

    = _____ + 2 = _____

11 x 3 = (10 x 3) + 3

    = __30__ + _____ = _____

11 x 4 = (10 x 4) + 4

    = _____ + 4 = _____

11 x 5 = (10 x _____) + 5

    = _____ + 5 = _____

11 x 6 = (10 x 6) + 6

    = _____ + _____ = _____

11 x 7 = (10 x _____) + 7

    = _____ + _____ = _____

11 x 8 = (10 x _____) + _____

    = _____ + _____ = _____

11 x 9 = (_____ x 9) + 9

    = _____ + 9 = _____

11 x 10 = (10 x 10) + 10

    = _____ + 10 = _____

11 x 11 = (10 x 11) + _____

    = __110__ + _____ = _____

11 x 12 = (10 x 12) + 12

    = _____ + _____ = _____

Try these!

11 x 15 = (10 x 15) + 15

    = _____ + _____ = _____

11 x 20 = (10 x _____) + _____

    = _____ + _____ = _____

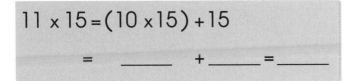

© School Zone Publishing Company

Delve into Twelves

You can use multiplication facts to describe groups.

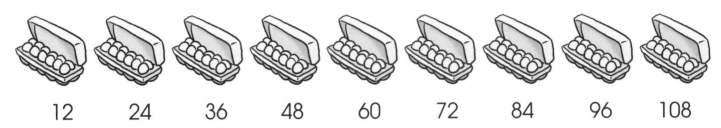

12 x 1	12 x 2	12 x 3	12 x 4	12 x 5	12 x 6	12 x 7	12 x 8	12 x 9
12	24	36	48	60	72	84	96	108

Multiply.

1. 12 x 2 = _____ **N**

2. 12 x 5 = _____ **O**

3. 12 x 4 = _____ **A**

4. 12 x 8 = _____ **I**

5. 12 x 1 = _____ **C**

6. 12 x 7 = _____ **E**

7. 12 x 6 = _____ **U**

8. 12 x 9 = _____ **R**

9. 12 x 3 = _____ **P**

Use your answers to decode the riddle below.
Write the letter for each answer on the correct blank.

What pine has the sharpest needles?

___ ___ ___ ___ ___ ___ ___ ___ ___ ___
48   36 60 108 12 72 36 96 24 84

10. Complete the table.

x	0	1	2	3	4	5	6	7	8	9
12										

© School Zone Publishing Company

Double the Sixes

If you know the 6 facts, you can double those products to learn the 12 facts.

Use the facts you know.

$12 \times 7 =$ _____

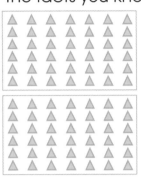

$6 \times 7 = 42$

and

$6 \times 7 = 42$

equals

$12 \times 7 = 84$

Write a pair of 4 facts you know to help you find these products.

1. $12 \times 9 = \underline{6} \times 9 =$ _____

   and _____ $\times 9 =$ _____

   So, $12 \times 9 =$ _____

2. $12 \times 8 = \underline{6} \times 8 =$ _____

   and _____ $\times 8 =$ _____

   So, $12 \times 8 =$ _____

3. $12 \times 11 = \underline{6} \times 11 =$ _____

   and _____ $\times$ _____ $=$ _____

   So, $12 \times 11 =$ _____

4. Practice the facts.

$12 \times 1 =$ _____ $12 \times 7 =$ _____

$12 \times 2 =$ _____ $12 \times 8 =$ _____

$12 \times 3 =$ _____ $12 \times 9 =$ _____

$12 \times 4 =$ _____ $12 \times 10 =$ _____

$12 \times 5 =$ _____ $12 \times 11 =$ _____

$12 \times 6 =$ _____ $12 \times 12 =$ _____

Count by twelves to check your answers. Or, you can add 12 to the previous product.

5. Practice the facts.

$12 \times 5 =$ _____ $7 \times 12 =$ _____ $12 \times 12 =$ _____ $9 \times 12 =$ _____

© School Zone Publishing Company

Dozens More

12 eggs = 1 dozen

Solve each problem.

1. John bought 3 dozen apples to make some pies. How many apples did he buy?

_____

2. Kevin is a dozen years old. How old is he?

_____

3. The third grade class planted 10 dozen trees on Arbor Day. How many trees did they plant?

_____

Did You Know?
A "baker's dozen" is 13.
(but 12 is the number used today.)

4. Kayla bought 3 dozen buttons. Then she bought 2 dozen more to complete her project. How many buttons did she buy?

_____

A gross is 12 dozen

Try These!

5. Jan's teacher bought a gross of pencils. How many pencils did she buy?

_____

6. Tennis balls are sold in cans of 3. How many cans of balls must you buy to have a dozen tennis balls?

_____

7. Some pairs of socks are sold in packages of 6. How many packages would you have to buy to have 3 dozen pairs of socks?

_____

8. Hot dog buns are sold in packages of 8. How many packages would you have to buy to have 4 dozen buns?

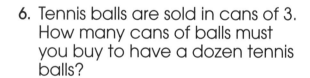

_____

© School Zone Publishing Company

Inches and Feet

Solve each problem.

1. Maria is 4 feet tall. How many inches tall is she?

   _____

2. Maria's brother is 6 feet tall. How many inches tall is he?

   _____

3. A yard is equal to 3 feet. How many inches are in 1 yard?

   _____

4. The flagpole in front of the school is 10 feet tall. How many inches high is the flagpole?

   _____

Try These! Hint: Draw a picture to help you solve a problem.

5. How many inches are around a 1-foot square tile?

   _____

6. How many inches are around a rectangle that is 3 feet long and 2 feet wide?

   _____

7. Ashton is 5 feet 3 inches tall. How many inches tall is she?

   _____

8. Jesse is 4 feet tall. His sister is 8 inches taller. His older brother is 4 inches taller than his sister. How tall is Jesse's older brother?

   _____

© School Zone Publishing Company

Who Am I?

Read each riddle. Write the answer.

1. I am 9 x 8 and 6 x 12.

   Who am I?_____

2. I am 3 x 8 and 4 x 6 and 2 x 12.

   Who am I?_____

3. I am 10 x 4 and 5 x 8.

   Who am I?_____

4. If you add 4 of me, you get 20.

   Who am I?_____

5. If you add 3 of me, you get the same answer as 6 x 5.

   Who am I?_____

6. If you multiply me by 5, you get 6 x 10.

   Who am I?_____

7. If you multiply me by 7 and then add 7 to the product, you get 6 x 7.

   Who am I?_____

8. If you multiply me by 9 and then add 7 to the product, you get 5 x 5.

   Who am I?_____

9. If you multiply me by 2 and then add 1 to the product, you get 9.

   Who am I?_____

10. If you add 5 of me and then add 5 more of me, you get 120.

    Who am I?_____

© School Zone Publishing Company

Home Run Hit

Multiply. Write the products in the puzzle.

Across

1. 11
   x 5

3. 7
   x 9

5. 3
   x 9

7. 8
   x 3

9. 9
   x 9

11. 6
    x 9

Down

2. 7
   x 8

4. 8
   x 4

6. 12
   x 6

8. 8
   x 6

10. 3
    x 5

12. 10
    x 4

© School Zone Publishing Company

Review multiplication facts 0-12   55

Multiplication Challenges

Solve each problem.

1. Seven bicycles are parked in front of the library. How many wheels are on all of the bicycles?

   _____

2. There are 3 spiders in a web. How many legs are there on all of the spiders?

   _____

3. If there are exactly 8 more weeks of the year left, how many days is that?

   _____

4. A small singing group calls itself "The Triple Trio." How many people are in the singing group?

   _____

5. Two baseball teams are playing ball. How many players is that?

   _____

6. How many fingers are on 8 hands?

   _____

7. Eight bugs are sitting on a lily pad. How many legs are on all the bugs?

   _____

8. Roger had 8 strikes in a row last week when he went bowling. How many pins did he knock down?

   _____

9. Rico wants to save some money each month in order to go to college 9 years from now. For how many months will he have to save money?

   _____

   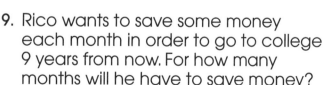

10. Six football teams are playing in a city park. How many players is that?

   _____

© School Zone Publishing Company

Multiplication Table

Complete the table.

X	0	1	2	3	4	5	6	7	8	9
0										
1										
2										
3										
4										
5										
6										
7										
8										
9										

© School Zone Publishing Company

Multiplication Table

Complete the table.

X	0	1	2	3	4	5	6	7	8	9	10	11	12
0													
1													
2													
3													
4													
5													
6													
7													
8													
9													
10													
11													
12													

© School Zone Publishing Company

Answer Key

Page 1

1. $5 + 5 = 10$
2 groups of $5 = 10$
$2 \times 5 = 10$

2. $3 + 3 + 3 + 3 = 12$
4 groups of $3 = 12$
$4 \times 3 = 12$

3. $3 + 3 + 3 = 9$
3 groups of $3 = 9$
$3 \times 3 = 9$

4. $3 + 3 + 3 + 3 + 3 = 15$
5 groups of $3 = 15$
$5 \times 3 = 15$

Page 2

1. $3 \times 4 = 12$
2. $4 \times 6 = 24$
3. $5 \times 2 = 10$
4. $4 \times 8 = 32$
5. $4 \times 5 = 20$
6. $3 \times 7 = 21$

Page 3

Check drawings.

1. $2 \times 4 = 8$
2. $5 \times 3 = 15$
3. $2 \times 3 = 6$
4. $3 \times 4 = 12$

Page 4

1. 16; $2 \times 8 = 16$
2. 15; $5 \times 3 = 15$
3. 28; $4 \times 7 = 28$
4. 18; $3 \times 6 = 18$
5. 20; $4 + 4 + 4 + 4 + 4 = 20$
6. 21; $7 + 7 + 7 = 21$

7.
Answers will vary. Possible answer: Multiplication is repeated addition, so the sum and product are the same.

Page 5

1. $2 + 2 + 2 + 2 + 2 + 2 = 12$
$6 \times 2 = 12$

2. $3 + 3 + 3 + 3 = 12$
$4 \times 3 = 12$

3. $2 + 2 + 2 + 2 + 2 = 10$
$5 \times 2 = 10$

4. $9 + 9 + 9 + 9 = 36$
$4 \times 9 = 36$

Page 6

1. 2, 4, 6, 8, 10, 12, 14, 16, 18, 20
2. 3, 6, 9, 12, 15, 18
3. 4, 8, 12, 16, 20
4. 5, 10, 15, 20

Page 8

1. 4
2. 16
3. 10
4. 14
5. 2
6. 12
7. 18
8. 6
9. 8

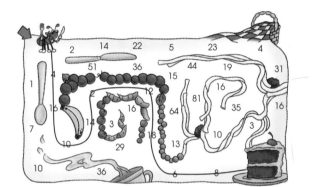

Page 7

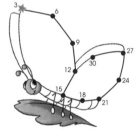
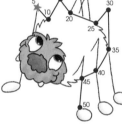
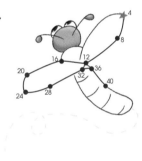

Page 9

1. 2, 4, 6, 8, 10, 12, 14, 16, 18
2. 8, 16, 10
2, 6, 4
18, 12, 16
14, 18, 12
3. 2, 4, 6, 8, or 0
4. 0, 2, 4, 6, 8, 10, 12, 14, 16, 18

Page 10

1. 15 **2.** 3 **3.** 12
4. 18 **5.** 24 **6.** 6
7. 21 **8.** 27 **9.** 9
10. $3 \times 5 = 15$
11. $3 \times 7 = 21$
12. $3 \times 6 = 18$
13. $3 \times 9 = 27$

Page 11

1. 3, 6, 9, 12, 15, 18, 21, 24, 27
2. 15, 24, 12
6, 3, 6
18, 27, 24
27, 21, 18
3. 0, 3, 6, 9, 12, 15, 18, 21, 24, 27
4. 18, 9, 3, 0, 6, 21, 12, 27, 15, 24

Page 12

1. $2 \times 4 = 8$
2. $3 \times 5 = 15$
3. $4 \times 6 = 24$
4. $3 \times 6 = 18$
5. $4 \times 2 = 8$
6. $5 \times 6 = 30$
7. Circle picture.
$2 \times 3 = 6$
8. Do not circle picture.
9. Circle picture
$2 \times 4 = 8$

Page 13

Check drawings.

1. 2 rows of 6; 12
2. 4 rows of 5; 20
3. 5 rows of 3; 15
4. 3 rows of 9; 27
5. 2 rows of 8; 16
6. 4 rows of 6; 24

Page 14

1. 4 rows of 5
$4 \times 5 = 20$
2. 4 rows of 7
$4 \times 7 = 28$
3. 4, 8, 12, 16, 20, 24, 28, 32, 36
4. 20, 12, 4, 28, 24, 36, 16, 32

Page 15

1. 4 **2.** 12 **3.** 28
4. 20 **5.** 36 **6.** 16
7. 24 **8.** 28 **9.** 8
10. A TENNIS BALL
11. 0, 4, 8, 12, 16, 20, 24, 28, 32, 36

Page 16

1. $5 \times 5\cent = 25\cent$
2. $6 \times 5\cent = 30\cent$
3. $3 \times 5\cent = 15\cent$
4. $7 \times 5\cent = 35\cent$
5. $4 \times 5\cent = 20\cent$
6. $8 \times 5\cent = 40\cent$

Page 17

1. 5, 10, 15, 20, 25, 30, 35, 40, 45
2. 15   5   25
40   30   10
35   30   20
45   20   35
3. 0 or 5
4. 0, 5, 10, 15, 20, 25, 30, 35, 40, 45

Page 18

1. 2, 4, 6, 8, 10, 12, 14, 16, 18
2. 3, 6, 9, 12, 15, 18, 21, 24, 27
3. 4, 8, 12, 16, 20, 24, 28, 32, 36
4. 5, 10, 15, 20, 25, 30, 35, 40, 45
5. 10, 20, 30, 40, 50, 60, 70, 80, 90

© School Zone Publishing Company

Answer Key

Page 19

Check circled groups
1. 5, 10, 15, 20, 25
2. 4, 8, 12, 16
3. 2, 4, 6, 8, 10, 12, 14, 16
4. 3, 6, 9, 12, 15

Page 20

1. 4 x 5 = 20
2. 5 x 4 = 20
3. 3 x 8 = 24
4. 2 x 6 = 12
5. 6 x 2 = 12
6. 8 x 3 = 24
7. Circle 3 rows of 6; 18
8. Circle 5 columns of 4; 20
9. Circle 6 columns of 5; 20

Page 21

1. 8;
2. 8;
3. 15;
4. 15;
5. 12;
6. 12;

Page 22

1. 1, 4, 1 x 4 = 4
2. 4, 0, 4 x 0 = 0
3. 8   4. 4
5. 0   6. 0
7. 7   8. 0
9. 6   10. 0
11. 0

Page 23

1. 0, 0, 0, 0, 0, 0, 0, 0, 0, 0
   0, 1, 2, 3, 4, 5, 6, 7, 8, 9
2. 0
3. that number
4. 3, 5, 8, 6, 4, 9
5. 0, 0, 0, 0, 0, 0
6. 5, 0, 4, 0, 0, 9, 0, 8
7. 0, 37, 43, 0, 60, 0, 74, 0

Page 24

8
1. 3, 2, 6
2. 5, 5, 25
3. 0, 1, 0
4. 2, 4, 8
5. 5, 0, 0
6. 4, 3, 12
7. 3, 3, 9
8. 1, 5, 5

Page 25

1.

x	0	1	2	3	4	5	6	7	8	9
0	0	0	0	0	0	0	0	0	0	0
1	0	1	2	3	4	5	6	7	8	9
2	0	2	4	6	8	10	12	14	16	18
3	0	3	6	9	12	15	18	21	24	27
4	0	4	8	12	16	20	24	28	32	36
5	0	5	10	15	20	25	30	35	40	45

2. 2, 4, 6, 8, or 0
3. 0, or 5
4. 0

5.
It is the same number as the second factor.
6.
15 and 15; 6 and 6;
Factors can be multiplied in any order to get the same product.

Page 26

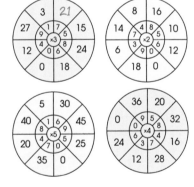

Page 27

1. 4; 28; 16
2. 2; 10; 18
3. 2; 16; 12

Page 28

6 x 4 = 24	3 x 3 = 9	6 x 9 = 54	3 x 6 = 18	6 x 7 = 42
6 x 6 = 36	5 x 9 = 45	0 x 6 = 0	3 x 9 = 27	1 x 6 = 6
4 x 6 = 24	1 x 7 = 7	5 x 6 = 30	5 x 7 = 35	6 x 9 = 54
6 x 6 = 12	6 x 3 = 18	6 x 8 = 48	1 x 9 = 9	6 x 2 = 12

0, 6, 12, 18, 24, 30, 36, 42, 48, 54

Page 29

1. 6 rows of 7; 6 x 7 = 42
2. 6 rows of 9; 6 x 9 = 54
3. 6, 12, 18, 24, 30, 36, 42, 48, 54
4. 30, 24, 6, 42, 48, 54, 18, 48

Page 30

1. 2 x 5 = 10 and 5 x 5 = 25
   So, 7 x 5 = 35
2. 3 x 7 = 21 and 4 x 7 = 28
   So, 7 x 7 = 49
3. 4 x 9 = 36 and 3 x 9 = 27
   So, 7 x 9 = 63
4. 7, 14, 21, 28, 35, 42, 49, 56, 63
5. 28, 21, 35, 7, 14, 42, 63, 42, 56
   0, 56, 14

Page 31

1. 28   2. 63   3. 14
4. 42   5. 21   6. 35
7. 0   8. 56   9. 49
A GOLDFISH
10. 0, 7, 14, 21, 28,
    35, 42, 49, 56, 63

Page 32

1. 12   2. 0
3. 16   4. 14
5. 20   6. 27
7. 24   8. 63
9. 25   10. 36
11. 28 12. 15

4	0	6	6	36	10	2	41
3	5	15	11	72	26	8	3
12	37	7	2	14	0	16	22
1	5	15	41	7	4	7	28
6	4	24	3	9	27	8	13
53	20	7	18	63	5	0	7
1	12	5	5	25	9	0	34

Number of Frogs	Number of Legs
2	8
3	12
4	16
5	20
6	24
7	28

Number of Flies	Number of Legs
2	12
3	18
4	24
5	30
6	36
7	42

60

© School Zone Publishing Company

Answer Key

Page 33

Across:
1. 35 **2.** 16 **3.** 56
5. 24 **6.** 32 **8.** 48
9. 14 **11.** 32 **12.** 0

Down:
1. 36 **2.** 14 **4.** 63
5. 28 **7.** 21 **8.** 42
10. 40

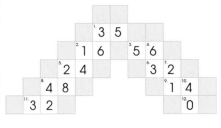

Page 34

1. 4 x 6 = 24 and 4 x 6 = 24
So, 8 x 6 = 48
2. 4 x 7 = 28 and 4 x 7 = 28
So, 8 x 7 = 56
3. 4 x 8 = 32 and 4 x 8 = 32
So, 8 x 8 = 64
4. 8, 16, 24, 32, 40, 48, 56, 64, 72
5. 24, 40, 16, 56, 8, 56, 72, 48,
72, 48, 0, 32

Page 35

1. 24 **2.** 48 **3.** 32
4. 64 **5.** 8 **6.** 72
7. 40 **8.** 56 **9.** 16
A BABY ELEPHANT
10. 0, 8, 16, 24, 32,
40, 48, 56, 64, 72

Page 36

1. 36, 3 + 6 = 9
2. 63, 6 + 3 = 9
3. 27, 2 + 7 = 9
4. 72, 7 + 2 = 9
5. 45, 4 + 5 = 9
6. 54, 5 + 4 = 9
7. 81, 8 + 1 = 9
8. 0, 9, 18, 27, 36,
45, 54, 63, 72, 81

Page 37

1. 27, 45, 63, 9, 72, 0, 54, 18
2. 36, 54, 27, 0, 45, 63, 81, 72

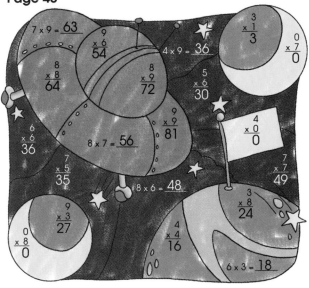

Page 38

x	0	1	2	3	4	5	6	7	8	9
0	0	0	0	0	0	0	0	0	0	0
1	0	1	2	3	4	5	6	7	8	9
2	0	2	4	6	8	10	12	14	16	18
3	0	3	6	9	12	15	18	21	24	27
4	0	4	8	12	16	20	24	28	32	36
5	0	5	10	15	20	25	30	35	40	45
6	0	6	12	18	24	30	36	42	48	54
7	0	7	14	21	28	35	42	49	56	63
8	0	8	16	24	32	40	48	56	64	72
9	0	9	18	27	36	45	54	63	72	81

Color these squares
1. 28 **2.** 18 **3.** 12 **4.** 40
5. 10 **6.** 18 **7.** 40 **8.** 28
9. 12 **10.** 42 **11.** 10 **12.** 42
A DIAMOND

Page 39

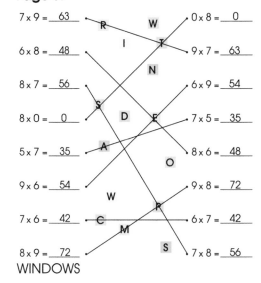

$7 \times 9 = \underline{63}$
$6 \times 8 = \underline{48}$
$8 \times 7 = \underline{56}$
$8 \times 0 = \underline{0}$
$5 \times 7 = \underline{35}$
$9 \times 6 = \underline{54}$
$7 \times 6 = \underline{42}$
$8 \times 9 = \underline{72}$

$0 \times 8 = \underline{0}$
$9 \times 7 = \underline{63}$
$6 \times 9 = \underline{54}$
$7 \times 5 = \underline{35}$
$8 \times 6 = \underline{48}$
$9 \times 8 = \underline{72}$
$6 \times 7 = \underline{42}$
$7 \times 8 = \underline{56}$

WINDOWS

Page 40

$7 \times 9 = \underline{63}$
$\begin{array}{r} 9 \\ \times 6 \\ \hline 54 \end{array}$
$4 \times 9 = \underline{36}$
$\begin{array}{r} 3 \\ \times 1 \\ \hline 3 \end{array}$
$\begin{array}{r} 0 \\ \times 7 \\ \hline 0 \end{array}$
$\begin{array}{r} 8 \\ \times 8 \\ \hline 64 \end{array}$
$\begin{array}{r} 8 \\ \times 9 \\ \hline 72 \end{array}$
$\begin{array}{r} 5 \\ \times 6 \\ \hline 30 \end{array}$
$\begin{array}{r} 6 \\ \times 6 \\ \hline 36 \end{array}$
$\begin{array}{r} 9 \\ \times 9 \\ \hline 81 \end{array}$
$8 \times 7 = \underline{56}$
$\begin{array}{r} 4 \\ \times 0 \\ \hline 0 \end{array}$
$\begin{array}{r} 7 \\ \times 5 \\ \hline 35 \end{array}$
$8 \times 6 = \underline{48}$
$\begin{array}{r} 7 \\ \times 7 \\ \hline 49 \end{array}$
$\begin{array}{r} 9 \\ \times 3 \\ \hline 27 \end{array}$
$\begin{array}{r} 0 \\ \times 8 \\ \hline 0 \end{array}$
$\begin{array}{r} 3 \\ \times 8 \\ \hline 24 \end{array}$
$\begin{array}{r} 4 \\ \times 4 \\ \hline 16 \end{array}$
$6 \times 3 = \underline{18}$

Page 41

1. 2 x 5 = 10, 2 x 6 = 12, 3 x 4 = 12,
2 x 7 = 14, 3 x 5 = 15, 2 x 8 = 16,
4 x 4 = 16, 2 x 9 = 18
2. 4 x 5 = 20, 3 x 7 = 21, 3 x 8 = 24,
4 x 6 = 24, 5 x 5 = 25, 3 x 9 = 27,
4 x 7 = 28
3. 5 x 6 = 30, 4 x 8 = 32, 5 x 7 = 35,
4 x 9 = 36, 6 x 6 = 36

4. 5 x 8 = 40, 6 x 7 = 42,
5 x 9 = 45,
6 x 8 = 48, 7 x 7 = 49
5. 6 x 9 = 54, 7 x 8 = 56
6. 7 x 9 = 63, 8 x 8 = 64
7. 8 x 9 = 72,
8. 9 x 9 = 81

Page 42

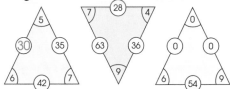
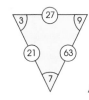
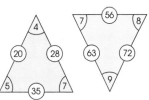

© School Zone Publishing Company

Answer Key

Page 43

1. 16, 20, 24, 21
2. 15, 24, 25, 32
3. 28, 36, 21, 48
4. 45, 6, 18, 36
5. 24, 14, 40, 56
6. 63, 64, 18, 0
7. 28, 54, 48, 63
8. 81, 0, 32, 54
9. 40, 49, 24, 56
10. 45, 35, 0, 72
11. 16, 42, 45, 28
12. 27, 0, 72, 0

Page 44

1-8. Factors may be in any order.
1. 2 x 4 2. 3 x 4 or 2 x 6 3. 4 x 7
4. 3 x 5 5. 2 x 9 or 3 x 6 6. 4 x 8
7. 2 x 8 or 4 x 4 8. 3 x 7
9. 28 10. 24 11. 45
12. 36 13. 48 14. 8
A RIVER

Page 45

1. 5 2. 6 3. 9 4. 6
5. 2 6. 3 7. 7 8. 4
9. 8 10. 9 11. 1 12. 8
A FLYING PIZZA

Page 46

1. 4 x 10¢ = 40¢
2. 7 x 10¢ = 70¢
3. 3 x 10¢ = 30¢
4. 6 x 10¢ = 60¢
5. 5 x 10¢ = 50¢
6. 8 x 10¢ = 80¢

Page 47

1. 10, 20, 30, 40, 50, 60, 70, 80, 90
2. 60, 40, 10, 30, 50, 80, 70, 0, 20, 90
3. 0
4. 0, 10, 20, 30, 40, 50, 60, 70, 80, 90
5. 100, 110, 120

Page 48

1. 33 2. 77 3. 99 4. 44
5. 22 6. 88 7. 55 8. 11
9. 0 10. 66

11	17	1	28	11	7	77
5	11	4	44	16	48	11
55	32	63	11	0	0	3
0	11	8	88	11	38	33
24	9	56	71	1	15	41
65	99	36	23	11	2	22
18	11	6	66	43	0	17

Complete table
0, 11, 22, 33, 44, 55, 66, 77, 88, 99

Try these!
$$11 \times 15 = (10 \times 15) + 15$$
$$= 150 + 15 = 165$$
$$11 \times 20 = (10 \times 20) + 20$$
$$= 200 + 20 = 220$$

Page 49

$$11 \times 1 = (10 \times 1) + 1$$
$$= 10 + 1 = 11$$
$$11 \times 2 = (10 \times 2) + 2$$
$$= 20 + 2 = 22$$
$$11 \times 3 = (10 \times 3) + 3$$
$$= 30 + 3 = 33$$
$$11 \times 4 = (10 \times 4) + 4$$
$$= 40 + 4 = 44$$

$$11 \times 5 = (10 \times 5) + 5$$
$$= 50 + 5 = 55$$
$$11 \times 6 = (10 \times 6) + 6$$
$$= 60 + 6 = 66$$
$$11 \times 7 = (10 \times 7) + 7$$
$$= 70 + 7 = 77$$
$$11 \times 8 = (10 \times 8) + 8$$
$$= 80 + 8 = 88$$

$$11 \times 9 = (10 \times 9) + 9$$
$$= 90 \times 9 = 99$$
$$11 \times 10 = (10 \times 10) + 10$$
$$= 100 + 10 = 110$$
$$11 \times 11 = (10 \times 11) + 11$$
$$= 110 + 11 = 121$$
$$11 \times 12 = (10 \times 12) + 12$$
$$= 120 + 12 = 132$$

Page 50

1. 24 2. 60 3. 48
4. 96 5. 12 6. 84
7. 72 8. 108 9. 36
A PORCUPINE
10. 0, 12, 24, 36, 48, 60, 72, 84, 96, 108

Page 51

1. 12 x 9 = 6 x 9 = 54 and 6 x 9 = 54 So, 12 x 9 = 108
2. 12 x 8 = 6 x 8 = 48 and 6 x 8 = 48 So, 12 x 8 = 96
3. 12 x 11 = 6 x 11 = 66 and 6 x 11 = 66 So, 12 x 11 = 132
4. 12, 24, 36, 48, 60, 72, 84, 96, 108, 120, 132, 144
5. 60, 84, 144, 108

Page 52

1. 36 apples
2. 12 years old
3. 120 trees
4. 60 buttons
5. 144 pencils
6. 4 cans
7. 6 packages
8. 6 packages

Page 53

1. 48 inches
2. 72 inches
3. 36 inches
4. 120 inches
5. 48 inches
6. 120 inches
7. 63 inches
8. 5 feet

Page 54

1. 72 2. 24
3. 40 4. 5
5. 10 6. 12
7. 5 8. 2
9. 4 10. 12

Page 55

Across:
1. 55 3. 63 5. 27
7. 24 9. 81 11. 54
Down:
2. 56 4. 32 6. 72
8. 48 10. 15 12. 40

Page 56

1. 7 x 2 = 14 wheels
2. 3 x 8 = 24 legs
3. 8 x 7 = 56 days
4. 3 x 3 = 9 people
5. 2 x 9 = 18 players
6. 8 x 5 = 40 fingers
7. 8 x 6 = 48 legs
8. 8 x 10 = 80 pins
9. 9 x 12 = 108 months
10. 6 x 11 = 66 players

Page 57

X	0	1	2	3	4	5	6	7	8	9
0	0	0	0	0	0	0	0	0	0	0
1	0	1	2	3	4	5	6	7	8	9
2	0	2	4	6	8	10	12	14	16	18
3	0	3	6	9	12	15	18	21	24	27
4	0	4	8	12	16	20	24	28	32	36
5	0	5	10	15	20	25	30	35	40	45
6	0	6	12	18	24	30	36	42	48	54
7	0	7	14	21	28	35	42	49	56	63
8	0	8	16	24	32	40	48	56	64	72
9	0	9	18	27	36	45	54	63	72	81

© School Zone Publishing Company

Answer Key

Page 58

X	0	1	2	3	4	5	6	7	8	9	10	11	12
0	0	0	0	0	0	0	0	0	0	0	0	0	0
1	0	1	2	3	4	5	6	7	8	9	10	11	12
2	0	2	4	6	8	10	12	14	16	18	20	22	24
3	0	3	6	9	12	15	18	21	24	27	30	33	36
4	0	4	8	12	16	20	24	28	32	36	40	44	48
5	0	5	10	15	20	25	30	35	40	45	50	55	60
6	0	6	12	18	24	30	36	42	48	54	60	66	72
7	0	7	14	21	28	35	42	49	56	63	70	77	84
8	0	8	16	24	32	40	48	56	64	72	80	88	96
9	0	9	18	27	36	45	54	63	72	81	90	99	108
10	0	10	20	30	40	50	60	70	80	90	100	110	120
11	0	11	22	33	44	55	66	77	88	99	110	121	132
12	0	12	24	36	48	60	72	84	96	108	120	132	144

© School Zone Publishing Company

Math Award

Great Job!

_____
Name

finished
Multiplication Facts Made Easy

from

School Zone Publishing.

 © School Zone Publishing Company   Multiplication Facts Made Easy **02214**